# 基于功能对等的商标词翻译研究

孙美玮 著

本书是山东省高等学校人文社会科学研究项目"概念整合理论视域的认知文体学研究"(J15WD03)阶段性研究成果。

苏州大学出版社

#### 图书在版编目(CIP)数据

基于功能对等的商标词翻译研究/孙美玮著. —苏州：苏州大学出版社,2015.9
 ISBN 978-7-5672-1461-3

Ⅰ.①基… Ⅱ.①孙… Ⅲ.①商标-英语-翻译-研究 Ⅳ.①H315.9

中国版本图书馆 CIP 数据核字(2015)第 199581 号

| | |
|---|---|
| 书　　名 | 基于功能对等的商标词翻译研究 |
| 作　　者 | 孙美玮 |
| 责任编辑 | 汤定军 |
| 策划编辑 | 汤定军 |
| 装帧设计 | 刘　俊 |
| 出版发行 | 苏州大学出版社(Soochow University Press) |
| 社　　址 | 苏州市十梓街 1 号　邮编：215006 |
| 印　　刷 | 苏州工业园区美柯乐制版印务有限责任公司 |
| 网　　址 | www.sudapress.com |
| 邮购热线 | 0512-67480030 |
| 销售热线 | 0512-65225020 |
| 开　　本 | 890mm×1240mm　1/32　印张：2.375　字数：62 千 |
| 版　　次 | 2015 年 9 月第 1 版 |
| 印　　次 | 2015 年 9 月第 1 次印刷 |
| 书　　号 | ISBN 978-7-5672-1461-3 |
| 定　　价 | 12.00 元 |

凡购本社图书发现印装错误，请与本社联系调换。服务热线：0512-65225020

# 前 言

《基于功能对等的商标词翻译研究》是一部研究商标词翻译的专著。商标词在企业文化及促进消费的过程中起着非常重要的作用。随着全球化的发展，越来越多的产品不再局限于国内的市场，而是走向了国际市场。产品能不能在这个国际市场上取得较好的效益，除了要求产品本身要有较好的实用价值和优良品质之外，还要看它给人的第一印象如何，而给人留下深刻的第一印象的关键就是商标。但是，一个商标在本国的受欢迎程度并不代表它在其他国家也能取得同样的效果，这就需要译者对商标进行恰当的翻译。对于译者，恰当得体的商标翻译是一个不小的挑战。然而，商标词的翻译不是简单的语言转化，它也是一种跨文化交际活动，它融合了多方面的知识，比如翻译理论、语言、文化、价值观念、宗教习俗、心理学、美学等。因此，对商标名翻译的研究，从某种意义上来说，就是一种文化范畴的研究。

在中英文商标互译的实践研究中，笔者注意到了一个奇怪的现象，即对英语商标汉译比较成功，而对中文商标的英译却错误频出。因此，考虑到目前研究的局限性和中文商标翻译研究的重要性，作者从语言文化的角度出发，提出用奈达的"功能对等"理论来指导中文商标英译的实践，并总结出多种基本翻译法以便更好地进行中文商标的英译，使读者特别是商标译者对中文商标词的翻译有个全面的了解，以收到较好的市场效果。

本研究以尤金·奈达的"功能对等"理论作为商标翻译必须遵循的基本原则。尤金·奈达是西方翻译理论界的代表,他的"功能对等"理论对翻译研究有着重大影响及指导意义。他认为,翻译是在译入语中用最切近、最自然的对等语再现原语的信息。本书在"功能对等"理论指导及大量英汉商标实例分析的基础上,总结出以下几种常用的基本翻译方法:(1)音译;(2)直译;(3)直译和音译相结合;(4)调整法。在商标翻译实践中,译者应灵活运用这些翻译方法,以期用最切近、最自然的对等语再现原始商标的信息,引起消费者的有益联想,激发他们的购买欲望。

　　总之,笔者希望通过对英汉商标翻译的系统论述为英汉商标翻译者提高商标翻译质量提供一定的帮助和指导,同时希望有更多的这方面的成果问世。

# CONTENTS

**Chapter One  Introduction**  / 1
  1.1  Background of the Study  / 1
  1.2  A Review of Studies on Trademark Translation in China  / 2
  1.3  The Layout of the Book  / 4

**Chapter Two  The Theoretical Foundations**  / 5
  2.1  The Relationship between Language and Culture  / 5
  2.2  Nida's Functional Equivalence  / 9
    2.2.1  An Overview of Nida's Functional Equivalence  / 9
    2.2.2  The Necessity of Nida's Theory on Trademark Translation  / 11

**Chapter Three  The Effect of Cultural Factors in Trademark Translation**  / 14
  3.1  Different Religious Beliefs  / 14
  3.2  Different Customs and Habits  / 16
  3.3  Different Thought Patterns and Concept Values  / 18
  3.4  Different Consumer Concepts  / 20
    3.4.1  Pursuing Good Luck  / 20
    3.4.2  Pursuing Elegance  / 22
  3.5  Different Psychology Structures  / 22
    3.5.1  Consumer Psychology  / 23
    3.5.2  Aesthetic Psychology  / 25

3.6　Cognitive Differences　/ 26
  3.6.1　Cognitive Differences of Trademark Translation toward Animals　/ 26
  3.6.2　Cognitive Differences of Trademark Translation toward Plants　/ 31
  3.6.3　Cognitive Differences of Trademark Translation in Color Preferences　/ 32
  3.6.4　Cultural Differences in Numbers　/ 35

**Chapter Four　The Strategies of Trademark Translation　/ 38**

4.1　Definition of Trademark　/ 38
4.2　Functions of Trademark　/ 39
4.3　The Strategies of Trademark Translation Based on "Functional Equivalence"　/ 41
  4.3.1　The Method of Chinese Pinyin　/ 42
  4.3.2　Transliteration　/ 43
  4.3.3　Free Translation　/ 46
  4.3.4　Literal Translation　/ 47
  4.3.5　Combination of Transliteration, Free Translation and Literal Translation　/ 50
  4.3.6　Creative Translation　/ 51

**Chapter Five　Conclusion　/ 54**

5.1　Conclusion of the Study　/ 54
5.2　Limitations of the Study　/ 56

**Bibliography** / 57

**Appendix Ⅰ Trademarks by Transliteration** / 60

**Appendix Ⅱ Trademarks by Free Translation** / 64

**Appendix Ⅲ Trademarks by Mixed Translation** / 65

**Appendix Ⅳ Trademarks by Creative Translation** / 66

后记　/ 67

# Chapter One

# Introduction

## ◆ 1.1 Background of the Study

The Chinese people don't really realize the importance of trademarks until the adoption of open and reform policy. Because more and more products are not only traded in domestic market, but also in different countries, since China has entered into WTO for many years, Chinese companies are exposed to the international market and meet fierce competition. Gradually, they have come to realize that trademark is one of their most valuable assets. Generally speaking, a good trademark should provide something about the product's characteristics—its benefits, use and so on. It's better to be simple in form and clear to spell, easy to pronounce, recognize and memorize. The most important is that it can improve its images and stimulate the potential consumers to buy products, which can bring a great number of sales and profits. Consequently, Chinese enterprises begin to make efforts to design their effective trademarks, especially the English versions. So the translation will play more and more important role in international communication. Whereas, in a different cultural background and advertising market, how to translate the trademark accurately which are admitted and accepted by potential customers is an essential question that the translators and marketers can't neglect. Trademark translation, in a broad sense, is a kind of translation; in a narrow sense, it is a special cultural transmission. A commodity's trademark is similar to human's name, which helps to differentiate one product from others and express many connotations and hopes. Meanwhile, it can protect a product's legal rights. The translated trademark is the second name of commodity in other country which should has the same function, so its importance is self-evident.

## 1.2 A Review of Studies on Trademark Translation in China

Trademark has quite a long history in China, and it was translated into Chinese since the day when foreign products and services entered into China. The first trademark appeared in the Northern Song Dynasty of China, which has its true sense in the world. In recent years, many translators have done many studies on trademark translation. But their researches still have some deficiencies. Until the 1980s, when China adopted the opening-up policy, the import of foreign goods began to increase year by year. However, until the 1990s, intensive researches on such translations appeared when China speeded up its economic integration with the world. From that time, many books and articles on trademark translation have been published. For example, Fan Yanbo (1992) wrote an article named "On the Chinese-English Translation of

Trademarks of Export Commodities", and He Chuansheng (1997) published a book *Brand Name English*, but they only contain some basic knowledge of trademark. Later on, many more articles about trademark translation have appeared. Among the articles about trademark translation, there are three authoritative translation journals in China—*Chinese Translators' Journal*, *Shanghai Science and Technology Translators' Journal* and *Chinese Science and Technology Translators' Journal*. These journals are always considered as high level journals and enjoy the biggest readership among both translators and translation scholars. Most of these articles have been dealing with the strategies and methods of trademark translation. Among all the studies, some translators have touched on the importance of culture in their essays. Zhu Xiaoju (1999) approaches trademark translation from the cultural differences, considering it very important to learn the Western customers' aesthetic conception and their response to the translated trademarks. Jiang Lei (2002) thinks that trademark is a part of one company's image which should stress on the expressive function and favorable association. He also puts forward the idea that overlooking cultural differences would cause pragmatic failures in the process of trademark translation. Hu Kaijie (2001) lays an emphasis on the importance of a suitable change of cultural connotation. Tang Degen (1997), Bao Huinan (2001), Xiao Hui and Tao Yukang (2000) all realize that the translator should take culture differences into consideration in trademark translation.

Though the previous researches have served as a starting point and have made enormous contributions to the research of trademark translation in China, they are still not enough. Therefore, considering the incomplete research and the necessity of Chinese trademarks translation study in the current situation, this book attempts to make a systematic study on Chinese-English trademark translation from the perspective of cultural differences, and introduces some Chinese-English trademarks translation strategies based on Nida's "functional equivalence" so as to provide a fine help for future study.

## 1.3 The Layout of the Book

The book is divided into five parts. Chapter One is the introduction which contains background of the study and review of studies on trademark translation in China. Chapter Two explains the theory foundation, involving the relationship of language and culture, Nida's functional equivalence theory and its necessity on trademark translation. Chapter Three analyzes the cultural differences of Chinese-English trademark translation in detail. Generally speaking, the differences contain religious beliefs, customs and habits, thought patterns and concept values, consumer concept, consumer psychology and aesthetics psychology, cognitive differences. Chapter Four analyzes trademark and its translation, from the perspective of cultural factors, introducing some basic information and translation strategies of trademark. In Chapter Five, the author comes to a conclusion and illustrates the limitations of this book. Trademark translation is a comprehensive subject, covering language, culture, beliefs, psychology and so on, besides translation methods. For translators, it is necessary to adopt proper methods so as to achieve the equivalence of trademarks in the largest degree.

# Chapter Two

# The Theoretical Foundations

## 2.1 The Relationship between Language and Culture

Translation is the inter-lingual communication (Nida 2001). In order to have a better comprehension of the process and essence of translation, it is always necessary and beneficial to understand the relationship between language and culture on the whole.

Culture is an abstract concept, which almost includes everything in the world. It has permeated into every corner of a society, and it also influences the translation of trademarks. Thus, considering target consumers' acceptance and their culture background is necessary when translators translate trademarks.

According to *The New Dictionary of Cultural Literacy*, culture is involved in attitudes, values, morals, law, art, beliefs and customs that distinguish one group of people from another. As early as 1952, American famous anthropologists Alfred Louis Kroeber and Clyde Kluckholm (1961: 181) had compiled a list of 164 definitions. Their lengthy (165th) contribution was as follow:

Culture consists of patterns, explicit and implicit, of and for behavior acquired and transmitted by symbols, constituting the distinctive achievement of human groups, including their embodiment in artifacts;the essential core of culture consists of traditional (i. e., historically derived and selected) ideas and especially their attached values. On one hand, culture systems may be considered as products of action, and as conditioning elements of future action on the other hand.

The word "culture" comes from the Latin "cultus", "cultivation", and "to till". Generally speaking, it refers to human activity. In academic study, "It refers to the total pattern of beliefs, customs, behavior, objects, and techniques that characterize the lifestyle of human being."

And then, what is language? An outstanding scholar, Leonard Bloomfield (1914) said, "Language is the medium by which people interact with each other and obtain some information from each other, which is regarded as a tool by human being to recognize and describe the world, and language is also the carrier and container of different cultures."

Language is the most important communication tool of the human being. In some sense, without language, it would be difficult to communicate each other. However, any kind of language is always linked closely with a certain culture.

Language is a part of the culture and reflects a certain culture, and plays an important role in culture. Some sociologists regard it as the basement of culture—no language, there is no culture. Inversely, culture also influences language. In other words, language reflects the characteristics of a nation, which not only involves the nation's

## Chapter Two
### The Theoretical Foundations

history and cultural background, but also contains the nation's customs, living habits, beliefs and thought patterns and so on. Language and culture influence and interact with each other. If people want to study a nation's language, they should also understand its culture; and, if people want to understand a nation's culture, they are sure to learn its language. Therefore, in the process of translation, it is important to understand and deal with the relationship between culture and language.

Chinese belongs to the Sino-Tibetan language family, and English belongs to the Anglo-Saxon language family, so there are many differences between the two languages as well as the cultures. From the geographical location, China and Britain are far distant and separated by vast oceans. There exist many differences in many aspects between the two countries, including climates, languages, living habits, social customs, historical background and so on. The particular culture of a nation is concretized and passed down through generations in the form of words and language. Thus, the cultural information shows many differences in the process of transmitting because of the influences of various factors.

Language as a part as well as the carrier of culture, it will certainly prove these differences. We have always thought that translation merely occurs between languages for many years. On one hand, this issue unleashed the word vs. sense debate in traditional theory and lied at the concept of equivalence. It is evident in dictionary definitions of translation. On the other hand, the Encyclopedia Britannica's contribution on translation does give cause for optimism: unlike the traditional way in linguistics (which endeavored to draw a sharp dividing line between language and "extra-linguistic reality for a long time"), language should not be regarded as an isolated phenomenon but as an main element of culture, while cultures are far more complicated than languages. A person can acquire a language in a few years through arduous efforts and proper ways, but it takes at least 20 years to become adequately acquainted with a culture (Nida 1998). "Language is essentially bound up with culture. It expresses, embodies, and symbolizes cultural reality." (Kramsch 1998: 3) Browmslaw Malinowski (as cited in Ogden & Richards), one of the first anthropologists, puts forward that language could only be understood in a certain cultural background. In 1923, he coined the term "context of situation" and realized that people could fully understood the "connotation" of a language when these two contexts (situation and culture) were implicitly or explicitly clear to the interlocutors and hearers. In 1911, a famous linguistic anthropologist, Franz Boas (1986: 7) broached the subject of culture and discussed the connections between language and the native environment. His main point was simply put as follow: "The form of the language will be molded by the nation of that culture."

Furthermore, Sapir (1949: 207) introduced his article on "Language, Race and Culture". He proposed that "Language is unique to human being, a symbol system with arbitrary created that communicates thoughts, feelings, and desires. It does not exist apart from culture". In addition, recently, NLP (Neuro Linguistic Program) has also taken the point that connotation in communication is culture-bound: "We know what things mean in our culture and the process of individual upbringing".

From the above mentioned, we can realize that culture is omnipresent and even mysterious and hard to acquire by the outsiders. An individual, who was born and brought up in a certain culture environment, can not completely understand that culture unless making great efforts. Furthermore, an individual who masters a certain language doesn't mean master the culture which the language belongs to.

In a word, Chinese language and English language belong to two distinctly different cultures because there are many differences in many aspects such as geographical location, living habits, social customs, religion, social and historical background, etc. So when translators translate the Chinese trademark into English, they should take the cultural factors into consideration.

## 2.2 Nida's Functional Equivalence

### 2.2.1 An Overview of Nida's Functional Equivalence

In the 1980s, some translation theories like Eugene A. Nida's functional equivalence theory were introduced into China. Nida has established his position as a specialist in translation after translating the *Bible*. In the process of translating the *Bible*, he found that there were socio-cultural differences among different countries and nationalities, and the need to make adjustment to the scripture is really essential. Later, this led to intercultural enlightenment. According to him, the concept of open-mindedness can improve human communication and understanding. Nida points out that translator should base on the establishment of cultural equivalence between the target language and the source language. He also puts forward that translators always apply his own personal values formed in his own culture and neglect the cultural differences in the translation, which is almost unavoidable; however, in order to translate accurately, a translator should firmly avoid personal factors.

Nida (2003) thinks that anything that can be said in one language can certainly be said in another. But to achieve an absolute equivalence in translation may be only ideal for all translators, because absolute equivalence in translation is impossible. In another book, he points out that "In such a translation, it is not so concerned with matching the receptor—language message with the source language message, but with the dynamic relationship, the translation should be substantially the same as that which existed in the original language" (Nida 2003).

In 1964, Nida puts forward two fundamental types of equivalence in the process of translation, namely, "formal equivalence" and "dynamic equivalence". Formal equivalence is text-oriented, which concentrates on the information itself both in text and form, while "dynamic equivalence is based on readers' response, it is another important contribution to translation research" (Ma 2003). Dynamic equivalence "shows a high degree correspondence between the source and target languages and embodies rather effective translating so that it can produce in receptors the capacity for a response very close to what the original readers experienced" (Nida 1993). Also, in another book *The Theory and Practice of Translation* (Nida 2003), he puts forward a more exact definition of dynamic equivalence, namely, "Dynamic equivalence is defined in terms of the degree in which the receptors of the information in the target language respond to it in virtually the same manner as the receptors in the original language". Obviously, Nida's theory stresses on the same response of the receptors in the target language and the source language. Later on, he divides the theory "functional equivalence" into two levels: the minimal level and the maximal level. The minimal level refers to that "the readers of the translated version should be able to understand it to the extent that they can imagine how the original readers understood and appreciated it" (Nida 2001). Anything less than this minimal degree of equivalence should not be acceptable. And the maximal level, the ideal definition of the theory "functional equivalence", refers to that "the readers of the translated version should be able to comprehend it and appreciate it in substantially the same manner as the original readers did". But the maximal level of equivalence is hard to achieve, if ever achieved, then the translated texts may have little or even no aesthetic value or may involve only routine information".

In a word, regardless of the minimal level or the maximal level, functional equivalence is the most important in trademark translation.

## 2.2.2 The Necessity of Nida's Theory on Trademark Translation

Just as Nida (2004) already said, "Translating is communicating, and this process depends on what is received by people hearing or reading a translation". Actually, the translator is promoting cultural communication. Translating is to express a text in another language. In fact, translation from one language to another is far more complicated, the reasons are as follows:(1) one word has more than one meaning; (2) many words are culture-bounded and have no direct equivalence in the target language; (3) a culture may not have the experiential background to permit translation of experiences from other cultures; (4) cultural orientation can render the direct translation into nonsense, so in the process of translation the translator has to take it into account and properly do with it and continue a kind of communication. It is very clear that translation and culture are indispensable. A successful translation can not only meet the equivalence in lexical meanings but convey the exact cultural information and consider the potential customers' response. Take "鲁班" as an example. In China, his story is quite familiar to people while Westerners know nothing about it. Therefore, if a translator translates it directly into "Luban", it is completely a failure. In other words, a good translation should make an adjustment or attach to some information so as to conform to the target language.

However, different people from different countries have their own understanding of words because of different cultures, which requires a translator to add some lost message or change the negative meanings into positive ones when they are necessary. Nida's theory is prominent for translation especially for cross-cultural translation. In his theory, he mainly emphasizes the response of the target readers. In the present book, the author adopts the point of view from Nida that readers of a translated text should be able to understand it to the point that they can conceive it how the original readers of the text must understand and appreciate it (Nida 1998). In a word, language is the medium of culture and reflects culture. Trademark translation plays as a communication bridge between the manufacturers and the potential consumers. Although trademarks are usually concise, they often contain some certain cultural information to show their characters, such as the trademark "杜康" (alcohol), the translation should interpret the cultural message and conform to the target culture in order that it is welcomed by potential consumers, so that the translation reaches the same effect in the target language as in the source language. That is to say, the prospective consumers can have the same response as those in the source language.

Thus, the process of trademark translation is not simply a process of finding equivalent expressions between the source language and the target language, but it also involves translating cultural image from the source culture to the target culture. There is no denying the fact that the translation of trademarks is quite a difficult task. However, judging the validity of a translation can not be restrained from comparing lexical meanings and cultural message, the response of the target consumers is also one important aspect, namely, the target consumers can understand and accepted it to the same extent as the original readers. Only when all these factors are considered, will the translated trademark be able to reach the effect, arouse the same interest and stimulate the same desire for the target consumers to purchase.

To sum up, Nida's functional equivalence theory can be regarded as the ultimate goal for Chinese-English trademark translation. As long as the translators apply this theory wisely and properly, we can overcome the cultural barriers and translate trademarks accurately through proper translating strategies.

# Chapter Three
# The Effect of Cultural Factors in Trademark Translation

As trademark translation is the product's link between two or more languages, and different languages represent different cultures, the trademark translators have to be aware of the cultural differences and keep high concentration on the possible barriers.

In this section, the author will analyze the effect of cultural factors in the process of trademark translation, which includes religious beliefs, customs and habits, thought patterns and concept values, consumer concept, consumer psychology and aesthetics psychology, cognitive differences, etc.

## ◆ 3.1 Different Religious Beliefs

A nation's religious belief is also an important part of culture. Of course, different countries have different religious beliefs. Thus, a nation's religious culture must influence widely and profoundly their language communication in life. The differences between the Chinese and British cultures are also bound to affect the verbal behavior and language notions. In China, the Confucianism, Buddhism and Taoism

## Chapter Three
### The Effect of Cultural Factors in Trademark Translation

are very popular. While British people believe in Christianity, they think that God creates the world. Thus, churches are very common in Britain, usually there is no food stored in church as a holy place. So in these churches, mice are often starving, which resulted in the idiom "as poor as a church mouse". In addition, British people firmly believe that God, heaven, hell and demon exist in the world because they are deeply influenced by the Bible. And there are many British idioms involving religious terms. Take the word "God" for example: "Thank God!", "My God!", "God bless me!", "God forbid!", "Play god.", "God knows!", "God damn you!", etc. Another example that comes from the Bible is "There is a bit of old Adam in us all". The "old Adam" is only a role in Bible, but it has been entitled with a certain cultural implication, meaning: "Adam, the first ancestor of human beings, betrayed the will of God out of the selfish and evil nature of human beings". However, since 1,000 years ago, Buddhism has been introduced into China, and it becomes more and more prevalent. So most Chinese people believe in Buddha, and it is very common to see many temples where people worship the Buddha by burning incense. So many Chinese idioms may contain such religious terms as Buddha, temple and monk. For instance, "借花献佛", "佛祖保佑", "菩萨心肠", "跑得了和尚, 跑不了庙", "放下屠刀立地成佛", etc. Many Chinese people would like to pray "菩萨保佑" when they are eager to gain success.

Just because of different beliefs, it often causes inconformity in trademark translation. Take "龙"(dragon), one symbol of China, for example. Of course, it is an imaginary animal. For Chinese people, everyone is proud of being the offspring of the Chinese dragon, and believes it can bring good fortune, and it is also the symbol of power. So many Chinese consumers feel like buying goods branded with "龙"(dragon), such as "飞龙"(flying dragon), "金龙"(golden dragon), "红金龙"(literally means the dragon is colored red and golden), and the similar are used as trademarks in China. However, Westerners will have a strong abomination to such trademarks; they almost don't use "dragon" as products' trademarks. Because in the West culture, even if "dragon" is only an imaginary animal, it does not arouse such a good association as it does in China. It is a symbol of fierce and brutal creature, and it refers to an evil monster which can spit fire and sometimes possesses three to nine heads. Though "dragon" is one of Chinese totems, we should not use it as products' trademark indiscriminately in Western countries.

## 3.2 Different Customs and Habits

Custom, as one of the parts of culture, reflects the specific characteristics of a nation or parts of the nation. It is the accumulation of long history and closely connected with the life surroundings and lifestyle. Some customs and habits exist in one culture the same as in another, so the same object in different culture contains different values and connotations. The difference also brings about an obstacle to Chinese-English trademark translation.

For example, "女儿红"(Daughter's Wine) or "状元酒" (Scholar's Wine), one of the most famous rice wines, is produced in Shaoxing, Zhejiang Province. In China, the two names represent the happy events in people's life, while it cannot arouse the same feeling

## Chapter Three
### The Effect of Cultural Factors in Trademark Translation

to the British. If the translator translates it literally, that will absolutely lead to cultural loss, because the British may not know the place Shaoxing, let alone the custom of the ancient place; on the other hand, they also don't know the story of "女儿红". It is said that in ancient Shaoxing, a jar of rice wine was buried under the ground when a daughter was born. When the girl grew up and became a bride, the hosts would dig out a jar and presented it to the guests who attended the wedding. As the jar was uncapped, the smell of the wine spread far quickly, all guests became excited and praised it, so it was named "女儿红". If the child was a boy, the family also buried a jar of wine under the ground, and they hoped that the boy could go to the top in the imperial examination, namely, "Zhuangyuan"(状元), who would be a superior official. After the boy passed the highest-level imperial examination of ancient China, they would also dig out a jar of wine. The story is passed down from generation to generation, from then, "女儿红" and "状元酒" have become famous trademark now. Thus, when a translator translate them, it is very important to convey the cultural information with the trademark. It is not difficult for customers to learn about the origin of the wine and accept it pleased, because any one from any country would like to enjoy the happy feeling and desire success.

Another typical example is the word "hare"(兔). In China, people always associate swiftness and agility with "hare", such as "静如处子,动如脱兔", which describes a person whose behavior is steady when remaining standstill but swift while taking action. But in Britain, "hare" is always the symbol of "cowardice", such as "as timid as a hare". However, as we all know, in ancient Chinese myth,

"玉兔" is a rabbit which accompanies the lady (嫦娥) under a bay tree in the Moon Palace. But for an outsider, one cannot associate the story of Chang'er who flies to the moon and lives there without mentioning Yutu. In a sense, in Chinese culture, Yutu is the symbol of the moon. So Chinese people like it and prefer to adopt "玉兔" to entitle their products which are related to the moon. However, if it is translated literally into "Jade Rabbit", foreign customers may not understand it. As a result, it had better be translated as "Moon Rabbit", which may be more easily accepted by foreigners.

## 3.3 Different Thought Patterns and Concept Values

It is well known that China has splendid culture with over 5,000 years' history and the different cultures between East and West makes people have different thought patterns. China is a nation that is conservative, subtle and modest, which is deeply influenced by Confucianism, while the Westerners are more candid and extrovert. The differences are also embodied in the process of Chinese and English trademarks translation. For instance, as we mentioned above, the Chinese trademark "红豆" (read bean—shirt) shows the yearning between lovers. Chinese people are very familiar with the old saying "红豆寄相思" (literally means to express the lovesickness with read bean), it represents love (Tang & Hu 2002:157). We can find out that's how Chinese people express love in a roundabout way. While some English trademarks, such as "Forget-Me-Not" (perfume), "Lovelift" (cosmetics), "Kiss Me" (lipstick), "Onsex" (women's underwear), "AMOUR" (perfume) express their affections directly.

Besides the differences of thought patterns, people's concept values are also different. Larry A. Samovar, Richards E. Porter & Lisa A. (2000: 60) said, "A value may be defined as an enduring belief that a specific mode of conduct or end-state of existence is personally or socially preferable to another." Jia Yuxin (1997: 59) thinks that the concept value is the instruction that people in any culture can't avoid the behavior standard, the thought patterns and cognitive criterion.

Chinese people have pride in their long history of tradition; they respect their ancestors and elders who are believed to have created history and brilliant culture. They are intelligent, diligent and sophisticated, so their views and advice have a great effect to the younger generation. Let's take "old" as an example. Chinese people would like to use "老"(old) to express their respect for their elders. And this concept value can be seen in many trademarks, such as "老爸"(Father—soybean curd), "老翁"(old man), "老干妈"(old nominal mother—food products), "老干爹"(old nominal father—food products), "王老吉"(old man who's called Wang—drink), "老人头"(clothes), "老板"(boss-ventilator), "泸州老窖"(a kind of alcoholic produced in Luzhou), "老北京"(shoe). These trademarks can easily arouse an agreeable feeling in Chinese consumers.

However, in Western countries, things are totally different. People always avoid using "old", and they hold the view that "old" means to be good-for-nothing and will soon die, so this kind of trademarks is seldom found in Western countries. They tend to look forward to future, youthfulness and new ideas instead of life experience, just as trademark of "Maidenform" (women's underwear) appeals to their desire to look young.

To sum up, almost everything which is related to the Chinese history and tradition is regarded as perfect and valuable. This is the reason why Chinese people often cherish the memory of the past, while Westerners prefer to pursue the future and the new trend (Li, Pan & Guo 2003: 99).

## 3.4　Different Consumer Concepts

The final purpose of trademark translation is to make the potential consumers accept products and promote sales. It is a kind of customer-oriented translation. Then, the consuming concept of people in target language becomes very important for translators to consider. In this section, we will discuss the differences of consuming concept.

### 3.4.1　Pursuing Good Luck

Chinese people like those characters that contain favorable meanings like luck, happiness, beauty, success, healthy and so forth. They think that these characters can express propitious, good and promising ideas. However, "It is evident that not only Chinese people but also people in any culture aspire to luck. In any culture, people think that language can bring in both good luck and bad luck. Thus, they hope to seek for beautiful things and pursue happiness". (Li Xiuqin 2001) The concept is also reflected in many trademarks.

For instance,"惠尔康"(drink) contains two concrete characters

and every word has its own meaning. They are of "cheap" and "health". The middle word "尔" has the same pronunciation of "而" in Chinese, which is a joining word. It means the drink not only has low price but also is a kind of healthy drink. In addition, "尔" also means "你" in Chinese. So "惠尔康" can be understood that this kind of drink will make you healthier. And in the trademark "康而寿", its characters "康" and "寿" mean "healthy" and "long lived". The middle word is also a joining word, and it hints "health" is a prediction of "longevity". Similarly, "安必信" can be explained that the product is safe and reliable, and you are sure to rely on it.

What's more, there are many Chinese trademarks that can express gook luck, such as "吉" (luck), "喜" (joy), "乐" (happiness), "佳" (fine, good), "美" (beauty), "益" (beneficial), "能" (capability, energetic), "健" (healthy), "顺" (smoothness, success), "富" (rich, abundant). These kinds of trademarks contain such characters, like "百事吉" (everything is lucky), "万家乐" (happy families), "吉百利" (luck and profit), "康发" (healthy and rich), "万利达" (profits pouring in from all sides), "喜之郎" (a happy man), "双喜" (double happiness), "健力宝" (healthy and vitality), "达能" (full of energy), "福满堂" (full of good luck), "福满多" (full of happiness), "美福乐" (beautiful, good luck and happy), "富贵鸟" (riches and honor), "永发" (make a fortune for one's whole life), "益寿" (be helpful for health) and so on. All of these trademarks express Chinese consumer concept of pursuing good objects.

### 3.4.2 Pursuing Elegance

With the competition of market, many trademarks, which are new and elegant, become more and more popular. Compared with former trademarks, those new trademarks are more elegant and attractive. Nowadays, with the improvement of people's living level, people not only seek for material satisfaction but also spiritual entertainment. They pay more and more attention to the beauty of trademark. Elegant trademarks become more and more popular. So in the process of trademark translation, the translator should consider this factor in order to entitle an elegant trademark.

For example, in "玉兰油", "玉兰" is one of Chinese favorite flowers. The two words "玉" and "兰" are usually used in girls' name. "玉兰油" can be explained to be elegant and full of fragrance, which may brings in a pretty imagination of girl's purity. This kind of trademark is often welcomed in the commodities used by women. They make good use of women's sentimental feelings and rich imagination. Some trademarks, like "雅芳", "飘柔", "舒蕾", "倩碧", are warmly welcomed by women, because these trademarks reflect women's grace and tenderness. (Li 2001) These elegant trademarks enrich both their lives and their spirits.

## ◆ 3.5 Different Psychology Structures

Psychology is a science, which studies the phenomena and laws of psychology activities. (Li & Qian 1995: 1) Psychological phenomena may contain sense and consciousness, which are relatively simple, and the comparatively complicated ones such as imagination, motivation, thought, interest, emotion, attention, will and personality. Psychological activities, including consumer psychology and aesthetic psychology, are closely related to understanding the meaning of trademarks.

### 3.5.1 Consumer Psychology

Consumer psychology, on one hand, means "the mental or psychological activities of consumers in their realization, adjustment of buying and consuming actions according to their own needs abilities under the influence of consumption and economy" (Gu 2002). On the other hand, it is a consumer's mental activities when he or she is purchasing or enjoying a certain type of commodity or service.

A consumer's psychology may contain two aspects: the social and the instinctive. The former is the responses of people's psychological activities according to the consuming surroundings and the general social economy. The latter is based on people's physical basements, referring to the responses and embodiment of people's psychological needs in a natural state.

For trademark translators as well as marketers, the possession and mastery of related information about consumer psychological are very important. To a great extent, whether customers like a trademark or not will influence their final decision of buying the product. That is to say, some potential customers may give up buying a product if they don't accept the product from psychology. Therefore, the translation of trademark must cohere with the reception psychology in the target market.

For example, in China, "水仙花" (narcissus) is respected as the flower with such noble characteristics as being clean and graceful that many manufactures want to adopt it in their trademarks. In contrast, Western consumers may associate it with the image of beautiful youth or excessive self-admiration, because "narcissus" comes from a beautiful youth whose name is Narcissus in Greek myth. It was said that a beautiful youth was in love with his reflection in water, died and was changed into a flower with his name. So it is the symbol of excessive self-admiration. Nowadays, we can imagine who will buy a product that is quite self-admired.

Also, we can take the color of "black" as an example. In the view of Chinese customers, it may be associated with being dirty, formal, solemn, etc. While in the view of Westerners, people always link it to disasters, such as the Black Tuesday, Black Friday, and Black market and so on. In China, a company produces a type of toothpaste named "黑妹", conveying the information that even a girl with black teeth can turn her teeth into white only if she uses the toothpaste. But we can imagine what reaction the product would bring about if it is translated as "Black Sister" literally? It is not only the symbol of disaster but also an offense to the Blacks.

In Chinese tradition, people use "帆船" as the trademark of carpet. When this product is exported to Western countries, it is once translated into "Junk". As a result, the sales are very unsatisfactory, because "Junk" is also the meaning "trash" besides "sail" in Western culture. But, who would like to buy "trash"? So it is translated as "Junco" (a kind of bird) later, and achieves perfect effect.

As we mentioned above, consumer psychology is a consumer's mental or psychological activities when they are purchasing or enjoying a particular type of goods or service. Consumer's responses to a trademark reflect their interests and favors. Normally, the image of a trademark will give hints to consumers' attitude, their likes and dislikes. So a perfect and successful trademark should meet consumer psychology need of consumers and make a good impression on consumers to achieve promotion effect of product.

### 3.5.2 Aesthetic Psychology

Besides consumer psychology, aesthetic psychology also plays an important role in the trademark translation, and the translated trademarks cannot make the consumer have the bad or negative association; otherwise, even a good product also cannot sell out well.

Take the trademark "纳爱斯"(detergent) as an example. Its pronunciation in Chinese creates certain beauty by rhyming. In Western countries, it is translated into "Nice", which is brief in form and sweet in meaning. Especially, the translated version meets the esthetic psychology of consumers in the target markets. Another example, the Chinese trademark "魄力"(chewing gum) is translated into "Sport Life". The name itself can be regarded as being delicate, elegant and powerful. At the same time, it completely conforms to the image which almost every one wants to keep healthy and strong in their inner heart. As a result, "Sport Life" successfully becomes popular in Western countries. In addition, it not only reproduces the closest natural equivalent of the original language information, but also embodies the esthetic characters.

To sum up, when translating trademarks, we have to avoid carefully the words which are disliked by consumers, and select the propitious names, making the trademarks more vivid, presenting the consumers with beautiful enjoyment and enhancing the expressiveness.

## 3.6 Cognitive Differences

As we may see in a great deal of trademarks, names of animals and plants, color words, and numbers are often used. But due to different culture values, beliefs and thought patterns, these words may contain different cognitive connotations for people in different cultures.

### 3.6.1 Cognitive Differences of Trademark Translation toward Animals

A lot of characters used in English trademarks come from the names of animals. In different cultures, the same animal may represent different meanings in cognitive field, sometimes even completely contrary meanings. Consequently, in translating trademarks with animal images, the translator should know about differences connoted by these animals. For example,

(1) Dragon

In Chinese culture, dragon is totem in Chinese history, and it is usually the symbol of great power and good luck. So many goods are named after it, like "红金龙"(Golden Dragon). However, in the view of British people, dragon is the symbol of crime and evil.

Therefore, generally speaking, Chinese trademarks containing "龙" had better not be translated literally, and it is always translated into "tiger" which represents power in Western countries instead of "dragon". For example, the translation of "金龙" (appliances), "Gold Tiger" will be more appropriate for Western consumers.

(2) Petrel

Chinese people think that a petrel represents bravery and fearlessness. The bird flies tenaciously in violent storms. The prose poem "Petrel" was written by Gorky, a well-known writer of Soviet Union, who has influenced the youth of China in a great degree. In China, the word "petrel" is used as trademarks for many products, like "海燕" heating shoes. But Westerners suppose the petrel hints disaster or violence. In their minds petrel represents those whose presence would stir up trouble in a social group. So the product which takes "海燕" as the trademark can not be translated into "petrel" directly. The translator needs to find out a sort of birds that symbolizes good luck in the cultural background of the target county so as to get cultural equivalence or similarity for the trademark.

(3) Peacock

In Chinese culture, the peacock "孔雀" is the bird symbolizing beauty and youth, because it is generally believed that the tail spreading of a peacock is a propitious sign. It is often used to describe beautiful people or things. In China, there is a story of "孔雀东南飞" (Pair Peacocks Flying Southeast) symbolizing love. In addition, in Yunnan Province, people of the Dai nationality pass down the custom of performing a kind of dance named "peacock dance" from generation to generation in order to express their good wishes for future life. So people would like to use "peacock" as the trademark of many products in China, like "孔雀牌" color TV set. While in English culture, a peacock is not a bird of luck, inversely, it is believed to be vanity, luxury and arrogance, describing a person who is always complacent and enjoys self-display. There is a saying of "as proud as a peacock" in English idioms. So it surely couldn't make the foreign consumers producing the same cognitive understanding as the Chinese do. Compared with "Peacock", the name "Kingbird" might be a better alternative, which avoids the adverse meanings and achieves the same effect.

(4) Phoenix

In the Chinese traditional concept, the "phoenix" is a bird with good luck, which will make people arouse the association of "good luck", "wishful", "noble"; therefore, many export commodities are registered with "凤凰" as trademarks or printing phoenix as a mark on the logo, like "凤凰" bicycles made in Shanghai. However, in English, it is said that this kind of bird builds blocks before dying, and regenerates from the ashes. So "phoenix" also means "regeneration", "resurrection". "凤凰" was ever translated into phoenix literally. People are bound to have the negative association of "reviving after dying" or "surviving" at the first sight. Obviously, such a translation is difficult to persuade people into buying the products in the foreign market.

(5) Magpie

A magpie is the symbol of auspiciousness in Chinese culture. If people hear a magpie's singing, it shows that happiness is coming. But in English magpie is often used to describe the sort of troublesome person who talks incessantly and tiresomely. In Scotland, a magpie's appearance means death; in Sweden, magpie is concerned with witchcrafts.

(6) Owl

In Western culture, the owl is occasionally used as trademarks, for instance, the trademark of a British publication is Owl. An owl is considered as an intelligent bird, and it is the symbol of wisdom. A proverb says "as wise as an owl". If anyone is considered owlish, that is to say, he or she is a very clever person. But as we all know, in China, the owl is the symbol of implying death and won't be used as products' trademarks.

(7) Cricket

In Chinese culture, the cricket is associated with a bleak and desolate scene with the coming of the autumn. In English, the cricket can be the merry livings in the extended sense and it represents happy life. There are English slangs "as lively as a cricket" (*Longman English-Chinese Dictionary of Contemporary* English 1988:335), "as merry as a cricket" and so on. So "cricket" is widely used as a trademark abroad such as "蟋蟀" automobile.

(8) Bat

Bat normally carries favorable association in China. The main reason is that in the word "蝙蝠","蝠"(fú) is pronounced the same as the word "福"(fú)(happiness) in "幸福"(happiness) and "洪福"(limitless blessing). So Chinese people believe it is the symbol of good luck, health and happiness. "蝙蝠"(bat) is a good trademark for a product such as Bat electric fan, glasses and so forth. However, in British folk legends the bat is an evil animal. And it is a wicked and blood-sucking creature which symbolizes something ugly. English idioms can give some explanation, like "as blind as a bat" and "as crazy as a bat". English people think that the bat is a blind ugly and fierce animal which flies only at night, and dare not to turn up in the daylight. In Britain, the bat stands for death, and if a bat comes into your house by accident, it may be an ill omen for you. Besides, the English people usually compare an old bat to an old blind and ugly woman. Can we imagine how the people wearing the "Bat" brand glasses feel? In the West, up to now, we still don't find such a product of adopting "bat" as a trademark.

(9) Goose

In China, "Goose" is a famous trademark for the down jackets because the double layer of this kind of jacket is stuffed with fine soft feather of the domestic birds. It reflects the first-class quality of the product. But if the trademark "鹅" is translated into "Goose", it is inappropriate for the down jackets. In Britain, the extended connotation of "goose" is fool, idiot and a blockhead fellow, as an English idiom "as stupid as a goose" shows the connotation.

(10) Crane

The crane represents good luck and longevity. Of course, the bird is favored among Chinese people. But in the West culture, the word means "adulteress". If "仙鹤牌 Tuo Tea" is exported to the Britain, the trademark can not be translated into "Crane Tea". Otherwise, it will find no market.

(11) Panda

As we all know, the panda is a very lovely animal and Chinese treasure. It is welcomed in many countries such as Japan, Britain,

US, etc. It is quite common to use "熊猫" as trademarks just like "熊猫" (telescope) and "小熊猫" (cigarette) in China. But in Islam countries, pandas are not favored because the animal has the appearance of a pig which is considered taboo.

### 3.6.2 Cognitive Differences of Trademark Translation toward Plants

Plant words also get different connotations to people from different cultures. People often associate their feelings and emotions, happenings and natural phenomena with various plants. For instance, in Chinese, "梅" (plum blossom) represents the noble, unyielding manner of a person (Guo 2000:335). So Chinese people feel like using it as trademark name just like the product "红梅" (sewing machines), but in English plum blossom is only a plant's name and does not have any other pragmatic connotation.

Besides, "松", "竹", "梅" are always called as "岁寒三友" (three friends in winter—the pine, the bamboo and the plum), which symbolize the lasting friendship in China. They symbolize the good virtue of durability. So "松", "竹" and "梅" are naturally welcomed as Chinese trademarks. However, in Britain, these plants give them no special sense.

"水仙" is often related to virtues like beauty and purity in Chinese culture, but the English word "narcissus" arouses an unfavorable cognitive association: self-center, ego, narcissism. Thus if the Chinese washing machine using such a trademark is exported to English-speaking countries, linguistic choices are very important in the cultural adaptation. Compared with "Narcissus", "Daffodil" might be a more suitable trademark name for it.

The three Chinese characters "紫罗兰" are the trademark of men's clothing. If it were to be put into Pancy, which also implies the effeminate man besides the meaning of a flowering herbaceous plant, it would not be a surprise that the clothing would find no buyers at all.

The following table compares the differences of some plants.

Table 3-1

| Chinese Trademark | Equivalent in English | Connotation in Chinese | Connotation in English |
|---|---|---|---|
| 兰花 | Orchid | Symbol of elegance and fragrance | Reproductive organ |
| 水仙 | Narcissus | Beauty and purity | Symbol of Narcissism |
| 百合花 | Lily | Noble | Bad luck and death |

As far as I am concerned, it is generally advisable that people should apply proper words to entitle their products, and when one translates existing trademarks of this type, cultural adaptation may help him in finding a more proper and accurate trademark.

## 3.6.3 Cognitive Differences of Trademark Translation in Color Preferences

As different culture causes different cognitive differences in different countries, this kind of differences also reflect in the different color preferences. As we know, different blends of the three basic colors, red, yellow and blue can produce various colors. Because of the three basic colors, people have a roughly common understanding. Even though people of different cultural backgrounds have the similar comprehension of the same colors, their feeling to the specific ones might be different, sometimes, even completely contradictory.

Take the color "red" as an example. In Chinese culture, "red" represents joy and auspicious, so many idiomatic usages with names of red are often heard. For instance, on wedding ceremonies, Chinese brides are dressed in red, and the bridegrooms' family people always wear red flower. In business, Chinese businessmen hope to make a good beginning (开门红). If business is prosperous the manager can share the profit bonus (分红利), and to the staff member who makes remarkable achievements in the work the employer would give him or her a red paper envelop containing money as a gift (发红包). Whereas, if a person is close to his or her superior, he or she will be called "红人". There are still many idioms connecting "red", like "红得发紫" (be at the height of one's power and influence), "红男绿女" (gaily dressed young men and women), "红白喜事" (red and white affairs—weddings and funerals), "红色娘子军" (red team of women), "大红鹰" (red eagle), "红蜻蜓" (red dragonfly), "红豹" (red leopard) (clothes), "红牛" (red bull) (beverage), "小红帽" (little red hat), and "红旗" (red flag), even our flag is red which represents the blood of revolutionary martyr, etc.

However, the peoples of English-speaking countries have thoroughly different cultural connotation for the red color from that of Chinese people. In Britain, "red" is used to express anger, cruelty, and lack of money in business, etc. We seldom see the Westerners use "red" trademarks in their products. If the manufactures want to occupy the international market, they must be aware of these cognitive differences so as to translate proper trademarks.

Another example is about the color "white". In China the white color means unfortunate and sorrowful because "white" is a word opposite to "red", and is the synonym of funeral arrangements. However, in Britain the white color represents loyalty in art and expresses hope in funeral services.

In English "white wine" does not mean the white spirit with high alcohol content but the grape wine. The English equivalent of the Chinese "白酒"（bai jiu）is liquor or spirits. Inversely, the Chinese "黄酒" can not be translated into "yellow wine" and English consumers will not understand even feel bewildered on seeing the expression. "黄酒" is made from rice or millet and emerges yellow with small amounts of alcohol content. As we know, Shaoxing, Zhejiang Province is well known for producing this kind of wine. So "黄酒" can be translate into "yellow rice wine" or "Shaoxing wine" which may be understood well by Westerners.

Let's simply compare some colors' connotation in China and Britain.

Table 3-2

| Colors | Chinese Connotation | English Connotation |
|---|---|---|
| Red | Joy, auspicious, happiness | Anger, violence |
| White | Unfortunate, sorrowful | Loyalty, hope, purity, elegance |
| Yellow | Honor, power | Shy, timid |
| Blue | Pure, relaxed and happy | Melancholy |
| Black | Death or terror, crime | Depression, bad heavyhearted, filthy |
| Green | New life and hopes | Short of knowledge or training, inexperience |
| Pink | Good luck | Essence, perfection |

From what we discussed about above, we realize that, if the translator only attempts to search for the corresponding words of the would-be translated terms based on the conceptual meaning in the target language without taking cultural influences into consideration, not only the cultural message can not be transmitted, but the translated terms might be not distinguished, even many ridiculous mistakes could be made.

### 3.6.4 Cultural Differences in Numbers

Generally speaking, in different countries, numbers also bring about different associations. Each culture has certain numbers which are believed to be either "lucky" or "ominous", but it may often differ from individual to individual. These differences are as follows:

As we all know, "thirteen" is often regarded as an unlucky number in the Western Countries. It is said that the number is concerned with a plot of Bible story, which says that Judas betrays Christ. So the number of "thirteen" is usually avoided in these countries. Any negligence of cultural differences would cause embarrassment. However, in traditional Chinese culture, the number "thirteen" does not contain the meaning in this sense, just as "王守义十三香" (spice), "十三叔" (foodstuff). However, in recent years, influenced by Western culture, some Chinese people, especially the youngsters, also begin to believe "thirteen" is an unlucky number.

"三枪牌" underwear which is produced in Shanghai is a famous trademark product and its English equivalent name is "Three Guns". If the underwear is exported to Japan, Colombia and North African areas, it will become greatly favored among these consumers, because "three" means activeness in these areas. But if it is exported to Chad or Benin, "三枪" cannot be translated into "Three Guns", because the odd number like "three" has the meaning of passiveness in Chad, and the number means witchcraft in Benin.

In northern parts of China, "four" means good luck, because it is an even number. But in many other places such as Shanghai and Guangdong "four" means a disgusting number, as it is believed that the pinyin (si) of "4" has the same pronunciation as "death". Under normal circumstances, the Japanese also avoids using the number for the same sake.

Sometimes, the number "five" is avoided by Westerners, especially "Friday" whose Chinese pronunciation contains "five". The reason is that this day is often called "Black Friday" when some awful events happen. But most Chinese people have not the same feeling towards the number such as "505 神功元气袋" (505 Shengong Yuanqi Dai), 555 (cigarette) and on.

The number "7" is thought to be a lucky number to many English speakers, because "seven" has positive meaning in Britain and European countries. A kind of beverage with the trademark "7-Up" is translated as "七喜" rather than "七上". In the eyes of the people of English-speaking countries, "seven" has the same connotation as "eight" in China. To them the number "seven" is a fortunate number and in hurling sport "seven" is regarded as the symbol of winning. The similar trademarks are "Mild Seven" (cigarette), "7-Eleven" (convenient chain stores). Generally speaking, "seven" is quite an ordinary number in China. But in recent years, many people use it in drinking hoping that they would make a progress in the future.

For a long time, the number "eight" has been favored in most areas, especially in southern areas of China, because it is pronounced similarly to "Fa" meaning "building up a family fortune" or "promoted to power and position". But in Britain "eight" does not have the same cultural meaning.

In traditional Chinese culture, "9" is the homophone of "久" which means "to last for ever", and it is often used to express the meaning of long time. The emperors worshipped "nine", hoping to enjoy lasting political stability. And the lovers like this number very much because they think it represents forever of their love. Therefore, China has the medicine "999" (cold medicine). But in English "nine" does not express the same meaning as that. Besides, in Western music and composition field, the number "nine" is a taboo, because the world-famous Beethoven died after composing nine symphonies, and composers like Schubert, Dvorak and Williams also passed away after finishing nine symphonies.

# Chapter Four

# The Strategies of Trademark Translation

## 4.1 Definition of Trademark

The trademark is closely linked with commodities, which deprives from and evolves with the development of economy. At the beginning, in Chinese there is not the word "trademark". In the past "trademark" was translated as "牌" (brand). Nowadays, it is generally translated as "商标". What does the word "trademark" mean specifically? It is a symbol, design, or distinctive coloring or lettering, which can't be vocalized. The definition by WIPO (World Intellectual Property Organization) is: The trademark is a sign that is used for identifying the products of an industry or a commercial company or a group.

Now many Chinese scholars and linguists focus their attention on the study of trademark. Some definitions of trademark are as follows:

(1) A sign (a picture, pattern or characters) on the surface or package of a commodity to distinguish it from the other goods of the same category. (*Modern Chinese Dictionary* 1996: 1104).

(2) A sign used by enterprises, institutions and individual entrepreneurs for producing, manufacturing, processing, selecting or

selling their products, generally expressed in characters, designs or combinations of the two, and usually marked on the product, the package, signboard and advertisements.

(3) A special mark that is placed on a particular brand of goods or commodity to distinguish it from similar goods sold by other producers. ( *Longman Dictionary of Commercial English* 1997: 791).

From the above definitions, there are some special characters.

1) It is the sign or mark on the surface of commodity or the package.

2) It is used to distinguish the goods from similar commodities.

3) The components are characters, patterns or the combination of the two.

The registered trademarks are protected by the law. The trademark registration protects the intellectual property of commodities. Generally speaking, to show a trademark has been registered, a sign of ® or TM is marked on the upper right corner of the product or the lower right one.

## 4.2 Functions of Trademark

Generally, the trademark is the core of a product's identity, which performs four functions:

(1) Attracting Consumers

A good trademark should not only provide with some information about the product, such as the place of production, the material of the products, but also attract the consumers. Thus, when designing a trademark, what designer thinks about is how to make the trademark more attractive to consumers. There is no doubt that the design of a trademark must be distinctive and unique in form from others, for example, Tip-Top (bread), Island Orchard (fruit juices) and so on.

(2) Product Identification

Nowadays, the prosperous market offers too many choices for consumers. A successful trademark standing for different manufactures is used to help consumers to identify different product quality, characteristics, prices, after-sales services, etc. In June 1975 a sample investigation was made among 1,000 housewives in Britain. The result of this research indicates that 50% of the goods they purchased were connected with trademarks. The trademark also helps assure consumers that they are getting comparable quality when they repurchase.

(3) Product Association

Some information which allows consumers to gain a general idea of a product can be conveyed from a trademark. For instance, "electronision" makes the consumer associate it with a kind of electronic apparatus, and "Hydromat" is a product related to water.

(4) Advertising Publicity

In modern society, the domestic and international markets have entered a time of abundance or even surplus of goods. In order to promote sales, advertising is the best choice. To some degree, people are likely to learn from advertising, imitating the latest life style. Trademark can be advertised and recognized when displayed on shelves in a store. The well-established image of a product has been printed in the brain of the consumers.

(5) Providing Legal Protection

Trademarks, especially famous trademarks, are valuable treasures for manufacturers and companies. Many countries have established laws and rules to protect their trademarks. The owner of a trademark is firmly protected against the use of the same mark, or a puzzle similar one, by anybody else on similar goods or services. For example, recently the group of "五粮液"(Wu Liang Ye) accuses of "七粮液"(Qi Liang Ye) adopting confusingly trademark name.

## 4.3 The Strategies of Trademark Translation Based on "Functional Equivalence"

Having discussed some basic knowledge about trademarks, language and cultural differences, now we will concentrate on how to successfully translate Chinese trademarks into English.

In translation, many methods are proved effective. At present, there are so many commodities in the market, sometimes we feel dazzled by the translation of trademarks. Trademark concerns image, credit, actual strength ... a series of important elements of company. According to William Wells, it is particularly difficult for international companies to adapt to product names in Chinese. For this reason, translating trademarks is really a hard task. However, if correct principles are followed and proper strategies are flexibly adopted, the cultural factors can be effectively overcome or reduced to a minimum degree to achieve the best effect, so that the products can get the greatest profit in the fierce market competition. According to Nida's "functional equivalence" theory, the methods of trademark translation are as follows.

### 4.3.1 The Method of Chinese Pinyin

Chinese Pinyin is a form of Latin words and the sound, meaning of Chinese. It is well known that using Chinese Pinyin is one of the translation methods, which is popular in Chinese trademark names, like Chunlan(春兰, air-conditioner), Changhong(长虹, TV set), Lining(李宁, sports wear), Jian Li Bao(beverage), Wahaha（娃哈哈, milk）, etc. Some use the abbreviation of Chinese Pinyin to express trademark：LL（露露）group, EMEI （峨眉）shirts, ZHONGHUA（中华）pencils, LC（浪潮）group. When Chinese Pinyin is used to translate trademark, the translator should realize that the mark itself has no sense and its meaning is the content of corresponding Chinese words. But some Chinese Pinyin words have connotation in some translation practices. For example,"芳芳"（lipstick）cosmetic's Pinyin is "Fang Fang", seeing the trademark, most Chinese consumers may immediately conceive of a young and beautiful girl. Although this product is of high quality, it failed in the Western market. While it is translated as "Fang Fang", "Fang" is "the poisonous teeth of snake" in English（Li 1996）. So what would the consumers think of when they were using the kind of lipstick with a terrible name? And there is a trademark "F·U·C·K"（pliers）. Maybe it is the abbreviation of a company's name. But "fuck" is also an English word which has the meaning "cheat, fraud", even "have sex" in slang. So when we use this method to translate, we have to be careful. The translation of "永芳"（cosmetic）supplies us some inspirations. "永芳" has been translated as "Yong Fang" to avoid ambiguity. Another typical example is the trademark "五粮液" (alcohol), which is translated into "Wu Liang Ye". We know that China is a great agricultural country in history, and "五粮" refers to five cereals including rice, two kinds of millet, wheat and bean. However, the Pinyin "Wu Liang Ye" does not convey any information to foreign consumers. But it is difficult for the translator to find an exact equivalence in the target language in designative meaning. While to Chinese consumers, the trademark has its associative connotation. It is the symbol of the cereal wine of high quality. It is said that the alcohol which is made of five cereals is the first-class. As a result, the foreign potential consumers who know nothing about it will hardly have the same response to the trademark as the Chinese people do. However, nowadays, this kind of alcohol just as "茅台" (Mao Tai) is very famous both in China and abroad. It is translated into "Wu Liang Ye" which is also accepted.

To sum up, Chinese Pinyin spelling is usually meaningless to those foreigners who do not understand Chinese at all. If we use this method to translate trademarks, we should avoid some difficult trademarks in pronunciation. For example, "正大青春宝" is translated as "Zheng Da Qing Chun Bao", "云山复方鲜竹沥" as "Yun Shan Fu Fang Xian Zhu Li", and "Shou Xi Hu" for "瘦西湖". Besides, these typical trademarks are also difficult for foreigners to remember.

## 4.3.2 Transliteration

Transliteration is often used to translate the trademark especially when the trademark can hardly find the correspondence in the target language. Transliteration needs the translator to take into account the sounds of words instead of their verbal meanings. Many trademarks of products from home and abroad do not have actual meanings. In cases that the original trademarks are not abstract, that is to say, they do not make sense to the customers literally, then transliteration is one of the best way to translate them. The strong point of using transliteration is that the translated trademark can best preserve the rhyme and rhythm of the original trademark, reflecting the commodities' special emotional appeal. (Bao 2001:285)

Besides, transliteration can remain the original flavor of trademarks and embody the country-of-origin or quality of products. For instance, "Honda"(本田) and "Sony"(索尼), two famous Japanese trademarks, convey customers a Japanese origin message, which reflects the high quality of the products so as to attract customers' attention. Another trademark K. F. C. (Kentucky fried chicken) also suggests that Kentucky State is the original place of fried chicken, which has the original taste. There are a great amount of examples of transliteration of trademarks.

The following table is some Chinese trademarks transliterated English versions:

Table 4-1

| Chinese Trademarks | English Versions |
| --- | --- |
| 康泰克(medicine) | Contac |
| 敌杀死(pesticide) | Desis |
| 强生(child skincare) | Johnson |
| 西泠(refrigerator) | Serene |

## Chapter Four
### The Strategies of Trademark Translation

(To be continuous)

| Chinese Trademarks | English Versions |
|---|---|
| 飞龙(medicine) | Pharon |
| 澳柯玛(refrigerator) | Aucma |
| 科龙(air-conditioner) | Kelon |
| 格力(air-conditioner) | Gree |
| 戴尔(computer) | Dell |
| 德赛(DVD) | Desay |
| 飞亚达(watch) | Flyta |
| 德生(radio) | Tecsun |
| 劳力士(watch) | Rolex |
| 西门子(electronics) | Siemens |
| 索尼(electronic product) | Sony |
| 锐步(shoes) | Reebok |
| 以纯(sportswear) | YISHION |
| 雷诺(automobile) | Renault |
| 马自达(automobile) | Mazda |
| 雪佛莱(automobile) | Chevrolet |
| 鄂尔多斯(clothing) | Erdos |
| 海尔(electric home appliances) | Haier |
| 方太(cooker) | Fotile |
| 轩尼诗(wine) | Hennessy |
| 摩托罗拉(mobile phone) | Motorola |
| 波导(cell phone) | BIRD |

Though this kind of translation is very easy to remember and sounds like its original name very much, it can hardly associate the feature of the product. Take "IKEA" for instance. It is a famous furniture trademark and its translation name "宜家" makes good use of the character "宜" meaning "appropriate for" and the word "家" meaning "home" to show that the furniture is very appropriate for your home. However, we can't know its quality from the name.

### 4.3.3　Free Translation

The meaning of free translation is that translators translate Chinese trademark into another word in English based on its original meaning. Free translation can well reflect the original purpose of the person who establishes the trademark. In addition, free translation can straightforwardly demonstrate the real sense functions contained in the original trademark and effects of products. It is feasible to make the potential consumers have a deep impression, or sometimes avoid certain embarrassing and unpleasant senses.

For instance, the literal meaning of "黑人" (toothpaste), a Chinese trademark, is black people. The trademark implies that if people use this kind of toothpaste, their teeth will become as white as the black people. So "黑人" was translated into "Darkie". However, the Westerners especially Africans may have a sense of racial discrimination of the word "darkie". Because of the improper association, it is better to translate "黑人" into "Darlie" replacing "Darkie". At first, it is short in form and easy to remember in sound; second, it can be accepted by the target consumers because there are no negative connotations in it.

So translators must understand the different associative connotations of words that have the same designative connotations. We must take the customer's cultural factors into consideration to ensure that the target consumers have the same or similar feeling with the original customers.

The following are some examples:

劲浪(chewing gum)—Cool Air
快意(air-conditioner)—Coolpoint
创维(TV)—Skyworth
娇爽(shampoo)—Hair Song
飞逸(shampoo)—Feather
双汇(ham)—Shineway
温雅(cosmetics)—Youngrace
统一(lubricating oil)—Monarch
戴梦得(jewelry)—Diamond
金鸡(alarm clock)—Golden Roster
朵彩(thermal underclothing)—Do Care
康莉(shoes)—Comrade
松鹤(medicine)—Long Life
堂皇(household textiles)—Shines

## 4.3.4 Literal Translation

Literal translation of trademarks, Bao Huinan (2001) explains, is to directly translate the literal meanings of the trademark. Literal translation means translating meanings literally, keeping both the original form and the original sense (Fang 2003:97). It is often used when the Chinese trademarks can find corresponding in English. The advantage is that it will be close to the source language trademark both in meaning and pronunciation and convey its exact original information and feelings directly and accurately. Although it is not suitable for every trademark to be translated literally, literal translation is still put to use by some foreign trademarks. For instance, the translation of "Mr. Juicy" into "果汁先生" can give customers very clear information that it is a trademark of a kind of fruit juice, while at the same time it also forms a cartoon image in people's mind. "Forever", a kind of bike, translated as "永久", expresses its special attributes or benefits. "Pioneer", an electronic appliance brand, translated as "先锋", can convey to the customers the information that it is the pioneer of the electronic appliance industry. Besides, "Microsoft", an American software giant enterprise, also uses this method to register its Chinese trademark. Translating "Micro" into "微" and "soft" into "软" successfully conveys the implied meaning: a basic, tiny and delicate software. "Soft & Clean" and "Breeze", two paper towel trademarks, are translated as "洁柔" and "清风" literally. "洁柔" conveys the original connotation of the trademark completely and meets people's requirements for paper towel, while "清风" arouses people's comfortable association brought by a breeze.

As far as I am concerned above, all of these translated trademarks are very suitable for their products. In short, we must make sure that the translated English versions must be acceptable in English culture and will not cause negative associations in the target market. Let's see some unsuccessful examples. "白猫", a kind of washing powder, implies the cookers and table ware can be washed as white and clean as the white cat. However, if translated into "White Cat", it is abbreviated into WC from "White Cat" at the beginning while the products are sold in foreign market. It seems like a joke, because people all know that "WC" is also the abbreviation of "Washing Closet". If it arouses this association to consumers, then the products can't be sold well.

For another example, "蜜蜂", the trademark for a bathing soap, was literally translated into "Bees". However, when the potential consumers from English-spoken countries see this trademark, they would be reminded of the tiny sting by the bees immediately. Who would like to cover the sting all over their bodies?

In addition, canvas shoes "大鹏" was translated into ROC as the trademark name. "大鹏" is a great bird in Chinese culture and "roc" is the same connotation in Mid-East myth. Of course, the translation is right literally. But if the word is used as a trademark, all three letters are capitalized as ROC, which happens to conform to the abbreviation of "Republic of China". So it is obvious that such mistake must be avoided.

Some successful examples of trademark translation are the following:

小天鹅 Little Swan (washing machine)
雪花 Snow (beer)
英雄 Hero (pen)
双星 Double Star (shoes)
新郎 Bridegroom (men's suit)
白猫 White Cat (detergent)
纳爱斯 Nice (soup)
金嗓子 Golden Throat (medicine)
现代 Modern (automobile)
猴王 Monkey King (candy)

天堂 Paradise（umbrella）

彩虹 Rainbow（clothing）

七匹狼 Septwolves（men's suit）

红苹果 Red Apple（jeans）

熊猫 Panda（TV set）

钻石 Diamond（watch）

将军 General（cigarette）

一支笔 A Pen（cigarette）

八喜 Eight Happiness（cigarette）

红锡包 Red Flake（cigarette）

## 4.3.5 Combination of Transliteration, Free Translation and Literal Translation

Apart from the above methods of trademark translation, we can also use combination of transliteration, free translation and literal translation as a trademark translation method to achieve the equivalence in function. The adoption of this method requires the English term should be capable of expressing the same meaning as the relevant meaning what the Chinese version means. In addition, this kind of trademark translation strategy is often adopted when the Chinese trademarks can find the correspondences in English which have the similar pronunciation. Therefore, the translated trademarks can be more attractive and acceptable by the potential consumers in the target market. A good translator needs to be proficient in both English and Chinese and to possess a perfect ability of art imagination. For instance, a sports shoes trademark "回力" is translated as "Warrior" because in Chinese "Hui Li"（回力）means the great power to conquer the difficulty. In English version, a warrior is a brave and strong soldier. Besides, the pronunciation of the two types of characters is quite similar. Naturally, a warrior who is very strong and powerful can save a desperate situation and anyone who wears the Warrior Sneaker would be endowed with such a wonderful energy and power. Wearing the shoes, the customer had stepped on a way to success. And the Chinese trademark "安秀" (women's clothes) is translated into "AN SHOW" instead of "AN SHOU". The Pinyin "shou" has the same pronunciation as the English word "show". In Chinese culture, "秀" means "elegant" and "pretty"; and the English word "show" is a verb which means exhibit. If it is used to mark women's clothes, it implies some one who wears the clothes will show the elegance, then she will become more beautiful, attractive and fashionable. As a result, we could accept the translated trademark "AN SHOW" has the same function as the original Chinese trademark "安秀". Some more examples are as follows: 哥弟(clothes) Girdear, 迪比特(cell phone) DBTEL, 唐狮(sportswear) Tonlion, 方正(computer) Founder, 斯达康(cell phone) UT Starcom, etc.

### 4.3.6  Creative Translation

Just as we have discussed in Chapter Three, trademark is a mainly culturally loaded. It is also a mirror of social culture. Trademark not only reflects the society, culture and customs, and meets people's psychological preference but also has an important influence on society, culture and psychology. Apart from the above five strategies of trademark translation, creative translation could be used as the complement of the previous techniques. This method often uses some of the characters and words instead of pure transliteration, such as addition or deletion of words, blending, acronym, and purposive misspelling.

Nowadays, the competition in the market is quite intense; a trademark with innovative ideas can help a manufacturer defeat his business rivals. This marketing strategy can get rid of the bondage from the original trademark in sound and sense, more vividly manifest the original trademark's features. The goal of creative translation is to remain the original trademark's characteristics and functions. For example, the translation of the famous trademark shampoo Rejoice is "飘柔", instead of "快乐" or "喜悦". The translator adopts the Chinese character "柔" which is only similar to the pronunciation of rejoice instead of its literal meaning, and this also may make consumers associate it with elegant and pliancy hair. The original English trademark of another world famous product "联想" in China is "Legend", which is changed into "Lenovo" later, instead of "Association", and it shows that the company is just like a legend and can make a great success. In addition, the pronunciation of "Legend" is more resounding than "Association", and has more positive meaning.

The most important feature of the Chinese trademark or the foreign trademark is concise and conspicuous, for it is easy to remember. The trademark of two or three English words or Chinese characters which are short and simple has some advantages. In this case, we can also adopt creative translation. For example, "飞鸽" (bicycle) should be translated as "Pigeon". There is no need to add

# Chapter Four
## The Strategies of Trademark Translation

"Flying" because "Pigeon" has the connotative meaning of "Flying" (飞).

Thus, creative translation can take the advantage of target language and make the translation conform to expressions of target language, and it produces surprising and prolonged defects through attracting consumers' attention, arousing their consuming desire and generating their consuming actions.

The following are a number of additional examples: "清逸" (shampoo) Ariar, "舒蕾" (shampoo) Slek, "滴露皂" (soap) Dettol, "法丝" (shampoo) Devos, "花王" (soap) Kao, "佳雪" (cosmetics) Cathy, "雅倩" (cosmetics) Arche, "美加净" (cosmetics) Maxam; "玉丽" (cosmetics) Effi, "臣功再欣" (drugs) Cuccess, "神奇" (drug) Maqik, "半球" (electronics) Peskoc, etc.

In short, in the process of trademark translation, one principle should always be remembered; the words of the final choice should be elegant and acceptable. The main purpose of the trademark is to deliver the nice information, and entertain the consumers with full enjoyment and promote the sales.

# Chapter Five

# Conclusion

## ◆ 5.1 Conclusion of the Study

Trademark is a special kind of linguistic signs. It is usually compact and concise in form and easy remembered in sound, whereas it is often heavily loaded with certain cultural information in content. That is to say, it is not only a trademark, but a representative of product, the goal of which is to attract customers and sell commodities. Therefore, the study of Chinese trademark is not only necessary but also urgent.

The translation of trademark is not a simple process, involving language, culture, marketing, translation strategies, etc. It is to stand for the consumers' acceptance culture, which can arouse consumers' interest and realize the value of products. As a translator, he or she should consider all the factors, especially the culture factor. To achieve the smooth transference of the cultural information, this book first provides the relationship between the language and culture. Language and culture are closely linked with each other. When translating trademarks, only the translator is familiar with the culture of the target country, can he or she fully convey the language message. And then, the writer proposes Nida's "functional equivalence" and emphasizes its necessity on trademark translation, and then puts forward that Nida's "functional equivalence" can be used as the theory foundation for trademark translation. In view of it, the author first produces the influence of culture factors in trademark translation concretely, including thought patterns, religious beliefs, customs and habits, and concept values, consumer concept, consumer psychology and aesthetics psychology, cognitive differences.

According to Nida's "functional equivalence" and the influence of culture factors, the author proposes six translation strategies: 1) the method of Chinese Pinyin; 2) transliteration; 3) free translation; 4) literal translation; 5) combination of transliteration, free translation and literal translation; 6) creative translation. No matter which strategy is used, the translator should consider the functions of trademarks and cultural factors which are the most essential elements in the translation process. Otherwise, the translation will not convey the connotations of the original trademarks and achieve perfect effect in the target markets.

To sum up, through the detailed analysis, we get a strong sense that although trademark translation is only a part of the whole marketing strategies of a company, it is a tool to connect the product with target consumers. While in the process of translation, neglecting cultural differences in trademark translation may cause translation disasters, even a great loss in the target market. Therefore, for translating a proper trademark, it is necessary to consider target consumers' culture in order to get the biggest benefits.

## 5.2 Limitations of the Study

Although the study has analyzed cultural factors and translation strategies in English translation of Chinese trademark concretely, it is not still far enough. First, the examples cited in this book are not rich enough. Second, owing to time and conditional limitations, the conclusion from the study is not testified by experiments and examination. Generally speaking, a scientific conclusion should be proved by experiments. So its limitations are quite obvious. The author hopes that this study can arouse more translators' interest and make further and scientific research.

# Bibliography

[1] Adam, J. H. *Longman Dictionary of Commercial English*. Shanghai: Shanghai Translation Press and Longman Asia Press, 1997.

[2] Alfred, L. K. & Clyde, K. Evolution and the theory of games. *Journal of Theoretical Biology*, 1961(1): 382 - 403.

[3] Charles, K. O. & Ivor, A. R. *The Meaning of Meaning*. London: Routledge & Kegan Paul, 1923.

[4] Claire, K. *Language and Culture*. Shanghai: Shanghai Foreign Language Education Press, 1998.

[5] Franz, B. *Language, Race and Culture*. Chicago: University of Chicago Press, 1947.

[6] Franz, B. *Tsimshian Indian Language*. Seattle: Shorey's Bookstore, 1986.

[7] Larry, A. S., Richard, E. P. & Lisa, A. *Stefani Communication between Cultures*. Beijing: Foreign Language Teaching and Research Press, 2000.

[8] Leonard, B. *An Introduction to the Study of Language*. New York: Henry Holt and Company, 1914.

[9] Linguistic Institute. *Modern Chinese Dictionary*. The Chinese Academy of Social Sciences (3rd ed), Commercial Affairs

Publishing House,1996.

[10] *Longman English-Chinese Dictionary of Contemporary English*. Hong Kong:Longman Group (Far-East),1988.

[11] Ma,H. J. *A Study on Nida's Translation Theory*. Beijing:Foreign Language and Research Press,2003.

[12] Nida, E. A. *Language,Culture and Translating*. Shanghai:Shanghai Foreign Language and Education Press,1993.

[13] Nida, E. A. *Language,Culture and Translating*. Inner Mongolia:Inner Mongolia University Press,1998.

[14] Nida, E. A. *Language, Culture: Context in Translating*. Shanghai:Shanghai Foreign Language and Education Press,2001.

[15] Nida, E. A. *The Theory and Practice of Translation*. Beijing:Foreign Language Teaching and Research Press,2003.

[16] Nida, E. A. *Language, Culture and Translating*. Shanghai:Shanghai Foreign Language Education Press,2004.

[17] William, W., John, B. & Sandra, E. M. *Advertising—Principles & Practice* (4th ed.). Beijing:Qinghua University Press,1999.

[18] 包惠南.文化语境与语言翻译.北京:中国对外翻译出版公司,2001.

[19] 邓炎昌,刘润清.语言与文化.北京:中国对外翻译出版公司,2001.

[20] 范彦博.浅谈我国出口商品商标的翻译.中国翻译,1992(1):14—16.

[21] 方梦之.译学辞典.上海:上海外语教育出版社,2003.

[22] 顾文均.顾客消费心理学.上海:同济大学出版社,2002.

[23] 郭建中.文化与翻译.北京:中国对外翻译出版公司,2000.

[24] 贺川生.商标英语.长沙:湖南大学出版社,1997.

[25] 胡开杰.试论商标名称英汉互译文化意义的转换.中国科技翻译,2001(4):23—26.

[26] 贾玉新.跨文化交际学.上海:上海外语教育出版社,1997.

[27] 蒋磊.文化差异与商标翻译的语用失误.中国科技翻译,2002(3):52—56.

[28] 李宝成.谈汉英商标翻译中的文化冲突现象.辽宁师专学报社会科学版,2004(3):95—96.

[29] 李贵升.论商标的翻译.中国科技翻译,1996(2):8—10.

[30] 李瑞琴,钱文亮.现代消费心理学.北京:中国商业出版社,1995.

[31] 李秀芹.外国商标词的转译方式及其文化心理.陕西师范大学学报,2001(5):308—309.

[32] 李延林,潘利锋,郭勇.英语文化翻译学教程.长沙:中南大学出版社,2003.

[33] 马艳玲.从文化差异的角度论商标的翻译.上海:上海外国语大学,2008.

[34] 佘艺玲.英汉商标名的文化差异与翻译.黎明职业大学学报,2001(9):63—67.

[35] 隋荣谊.英汉翻译新教程.北京:中国电力出版社,2004.

[36] 唐德根.文化差异在品牌翻译中的运用.上海科技翻译,1997(1):24—27.

[37] 唐忠顺,胡剑波.从跨文化交际看商标词的翻译.中国矿业大学学报(社会科学版),2002(1):155—160.

[38] 肖辉,陶玉康.等效原则视角下的商标翻译与文化联想.外语与外语教学,2000(1):51—53.

[39] 朱小菊.出口商品名称和商标的翻译.中国科技翻译,1999(2):49—52.

# Appendix I
# Trademarks by Transliteration

| | | | |
|---|---|---|---|
| Adidas | 阿迪达斯 | BOSIDENG | 波司登 |
| AIDUNNI | 爱敦尼 | Bossini | 堡狮龙 |
| Aimer | 爱慕 | Burberry | 巴巴利 |
| Aline | 阿莱 | BUT | 布同 |
| AN SHOW | 安秀 | Bvlgari | 宝格丽 |
| ANJEWEL | 安伽罗 | Cabbeen | 卡宾 |
| Anta | 安踏 | Castle | 卡索 |
| Amani | 阿玛尼 | CANUDILO | 卡奴迪路 |
| AROMATNE | 艾洛曼妮 | Carbanni | 卡邦尼 |
| Asics | 爱世克斯 | Cannen | 卡蔓 |
| AZONA | 阿桑娜 | Cartier | 卡蒂亚 |
| Babala | 芭芭拉 | Chanel | 香奈尔 |
| Baleno | 班尼路 | Christian Dior | 迪奥 |
| BaoXiNiao | 报喜鸟 | CKEVIN | 寇吻 |
| Be Born | 碧邦 | CONCENT | 康先特 |
| BeiDanNa | 贝丹娜 | COONIC | 珂妮卡 |
| Belle | 百丽 | CORONA | 珂罗娜 |
| BIEDK | 贝尔丹格 | Dai Shu | 袋鼠 |
| BONI | 堡尼 | DaPhne | 达芙妮 |

| | | | |
|---|---|---|---|
| Deff Landy | 黛芙兰蒂 | gongfu | 功夫牌轻便鞋 |
| DEICAE | 迪赛 | Goodwill | 高登威尔 |
| Devino | 迪威诺 | Gucci | 古奇 |
| DIDIBOY | 迪迪博迩 | GUZZNO | 古希诺 |
| DIKENI | 迪柯尼 | Gvein | 古恩 |
| Donna Karan | 唐纳·卡兰 | Hermes | 爱马仕 |
| EAST SHOW | 伊斯特秀 | HOLY—G | 好理吉 |
| Ebase | 衣本色 | HUANUOWEI | 华诺威 |
| EE edela | 埃迪拉 | Jaccos | 积高 |
| Eitie | 爱特爱 | Jack & Jones | 杰克琼斯 |
| ELLFISH | 艾尔霏思 | Jackwalk | 杰克沃克 |
| ema | 爱玛 | Jameshans | 杰尼轩诗 |
| EsPrit | 爱使普利 | JARCA | 捷卡 |
| FAPAI | 法派 | JEFEN | 吉芬 |
| Fay—Fayee | 费依 | JESSICA | 杰西卡 |
| Fecie | 芬狄诗 | JEVAROSA | 洁菲洛迎 |
| Fendi | 芬迪 | JIEHAO | 杰豪 |
| Fila | 斐乐 | JIMANNO | 纪曼诺 |
| Finity | 菲妮迪 | KLOVA | 柯罗芭 |
| Florid | 芙罗迪 | KOREANO | 柯利亚诺 |
| FRNDO | 菲尔南多 | KYLIMINO | 凯莉米洛 |
| GEMANS | 格漫诗 | La vieo | 朗维高 |
| GEYAO | 歌谣 | Lancy | 朗姿 |
| Giordano | 佐丹奴 | LANBNA | 兰毕安 |
| GIRDEAR | 哥弟 | LANIWEIGE | 莱妮薇格 |
| Givenchy | 纪梵希 | LE SHEMYA | 来尔雷米雅 |
| Gloria | 歌莉娅 | Lee | 利 |

| | | | |
|---|---|---|---|
| Lerario | 赖尔利奥 | MYFILED | 玛菲迪 |
| LEVARIA | 璐·维莎 | OASIS | 奥诗裳 |
| Levi's | 李维 | Ochirly | 欧时力 |
| LiNing | 李宁 | ORLLIER | 奥丽尔 |
| Lilang | 利郎 | OSTIN | 奥诗丹 |
| LIOU | 骊欧 | OSULOR | 澳狮龙 |
| LOEWE | 罗威 | Ourlilae | 奥韵莱 |
| Louis Cardi | 路易卡迪 | Palieli | 芭黎金领 |
| Louis Vuitton | 路易·威登 | Pierre cardin | 皮尔·卡丹 |
| LOYER | 容悦 | PORTS | 宝姿 |
| LUCY | 茹西 | Prada | 普拉达 |
| Nannar | 纳琪 | Rhema | 丙玛 |
| NEMOW | 南梦 | ROMON | 罗蒙 |
| NEPTUNE | 尼普顿 | SainiNadia | 圣·娜迪雅 |
| Nike | 耐克 | S. DEER | 圣迪奥 |
| Nina Ricci | 尼娜·里奇 | Sefo | 臣枫 |
| Mailyard | 美尔雅 | Semir | 森马 |
| maru | 宾汉 | SENDA | 森达 |
| Max Maria | 玛思玛丽 | Sfenth | 诗凡诗 |
| MaxFaerie | 玛丝菲瑞 | SIDYAWEN | 丝蒂雅文 |
| Maxico | 玛诗可 | SIEGO | 西范 |
| MEDORIA | 美多利亚 | SINA COVA | 辛纳克尔 |
| Metersbonwe | 美特斯邦威 | SITTON | 仕登 |
| MEYER | 迈雅 | Stovenno | 斯托梵诺 |
| Mimi | 咪咪 | SUNDANCE | 圣得西 |
| MJIAM | 美加美 | TAHAN | 太和 |
| MOCANO | 摩卡奴 | TANOY | 天意 |

| | | | |
|---|---|---|---|
| teenieweenie | 维尼熊 | VOVOS | 微微思 |
| TEMAR | 泰玛 | WE WANT | 维温 |
| TERESIA | 特蕾西娅 | WeiPeng | 威鹏 |
| TONY WEAR | 汤尼威尔 | WIELll | 威利 |
| UNIKON | 尤尼可 | XUEGE | 雪歌 |
| Valentino | 瓦伦蒂诺 | YIFINl | 易菲 |
| VASTO | 华斯度 | YIGUE | 亦谷 |
| VEEKO | 威高 | Yishion | 以纯 |
| Versace | 范思哲 | Youngor | 雅戈尔 |

# Appendix II
## Trademarks by Free Translation

| | | | |
|---|---|---|---|
| A&Y | 爱唯 | Hanace Mori | 森英惠 |
| ANY—ALL | 必然 | i'LL-Zoni | 艾菲桑妮 |
| Balenciaga | 巴黎世家 | Joy&Peace | 真美诗 |
| BBLLUUEE | 粉蓝 | KNOWN | 人和 |
| BIYO | 魅力尚品 | LAUDAT10N | 蓝天龙 |
| BUT | 布同 | Love bean | 红豆 |
| Change she | 千细 | NowHere | 艾希尔 |
| E&YOU | 伊可爱 | POLO | 马球 |
| FAITIME | 习卜 | SHOW TIME LI | 逸妃 |
| FANSKY | 反思 | SIMTLY | 纯粹 |
| First View | 秋水伊人 | STRONG HORSE | 喜尔斯 |
| FLEUO | 尚沐 | Take it | 艾衣人 |
| FRANCEPAL | 龙虾 | Theme | 荣晖 |
| Girl line | 格子廊 | Vocci Eva | 兰林 |
| Gracewell | 婷美 | W—tu | 空间 |
| Great | 格威特 | ZAVA | 致魅 |

# Appendix III
## Trademarks by Mixed Translation

| | | | |
|---|---|---|---|
| A. MODERN | 爱·摩登 | K. KENNY | 扣扣 |
| ACTARIS | 阿驼力 | KAKO | 慧中 |
| Amelie | 奢爱 | K-boxing | 劲霸 |
| BABY FOX | 诱狐 | LITHIAR | 丽想 |
| E-land | 依恋 | Mark Fairwhale | 马克华菲 |
| Etam | 艾格 | MOCOME | 魔范 |
| FINETTE | 纷丽 | Mysheros | 蜜雪儿 |
| G. yose | 金优子 | Only& One | 唯依 |
| GIORZIO | 玖姿 | Q. BSMART | 情报站 |
| Goldlion | 金利来 | Radarbird | 雷鸟 |
| HAVE HILL | 德峰 | Reebok | 锐步 |
| HON. B | 红贝堤 | Total | 统统 |
| HONRN | 红人 | Warrior | 回力 |
| JOEONE | 九牧王 | ZERONINTY-NINE | 零点久久 |

# Appendix IV
# Trademarks by Creative Translation

| | | | |
|---|---|---|---|
| BIANCO | 范怡文 | KNITNET | 妮珂爱 |
| Embry Form | 安莉芳 | Little Bobdog | 巴不豆 |
| Erdos | 鄂尔多斯 | Marie France | 玛莉法兰 |
| Hasbro | 孩之宝 | SUSSI | 古色 |
| Hillo | 雄山 | Triumph | 黛安芬 |
| In see | 上格 | VERO MODA | 维沙曼 |
| Junk | 帆船 | | |

# 后 记

《基于功能对等的商标词翻译研究》一书就要付梓了,多年的研究成果终于要和读者见面了。可是心中总是忐忑不安,读者将如何评价这本书呢？这种不安的心情贯穿了此项研究的始终,可能是因为能力有限,也可能是对研究工作的要求近似苛求。即使是现在,脑海深处泛起的也只有那漫漫长夜中苦苦的思索,那久坐案头引发的身体的不适,那在睡梦中奋笔疾书醒来却两手空空的恼恨。

但最终这本书得以出版,应归功于在不同阶段以不同方式帮助过我的老师、同事、朋友及家人。我知道这小小的后记容不下我对他们的感激之情,但我还是要把他们一一提起。只有这样的回忆才会唤起我在艰辛的研究过程中享受到的快乐。

首先我要感谢我的导师、曲阜师范大学外国语学院的王广成教授,是他引领我走上学术研究的道路。在研究的过程中,他一直给予我指导和帮助,并为该研究奠定了良好的基础。我至今仍深深记得他给我们带来的诸多的研究资料。

我要感谢菏泽学院外国语系的何常丽副教授、李运河副教授。在我的研究过程中,他们以不同的方式提出各种建议和意见,不仅开阔了我的视野,也丰富、深化了本书的结构,使这项研究增色不少。

最后我要感谢我的家人。感谢我的父母,感谢他们对我的大力支持和理解！感谢我的丈夫司景方一直鼓励我积极进取、专心读书。

  本书得到了菏泽学院外国语系及科研处领导的关心和支持。本书得以出版更离不开苏州大学出版社的大力支持，汤定军先生为拙作提供了很多建议，在此一并感谢。

  尽管本书在选题和撰写的过程中得到了诸多的帮助，但我的学识与能力有限，难免出现谬误，在具体的论证过程中出现的错误和误解皆由本人才疏学浅所致，恳请读者批评指正。

孙美玮

2015 年 1 月 24 日于菏泽